Dedication

To my grandparents and parents, who believed in a reality of greater opportunity and rigorously paved the way for me to see a world of choice.

To my precious friends and mentors, my additional family, who live unapologetically in their expression— encouraging me to find a safety and FUN in choosing to honor my own truth.

To the artists, divinely encounters, and <u>you</u>, who fill the world with your distinct and timely voices that incite change.

A note for you.

Dearest,

One thing I believe and will remind you of is that your presence alone alters the world for the better. Your unique self- your distinct vibration- can evolve existence as a whole. You being you has the power to change the world and does change the world through the ripple effect you continuously have.

With that being said, expressing yourself- embodying your voice- cannot possibly be done "wrong." Your voice is your own expression, and nobody can replace that; nobody can take that away from you.

So, how can you can use your voice to inspire change in the world? I say that the simple answer is to just use your voice. When you embrace yourself, when you choose to honor where internal joy points you toward, it viscerally guides you on how to embody what truthful alignment looks like for you.

There is no expression of you that is too loud, and there is no way to not be heard when you allow the beauty of who you are to audibly radiate out from you. Your truth has the capacity to drive a population, to harmonize a crowd, to create a sense of solidarity.

You receiving your voice is the authenticity which ignites the voices, vulnerability, and rooted connection in others. I know this, because this is what inspires me everyday. Individual's presences, passions, and inner-power is what catalyzes a safety in my own self to speak up and not dim my light.

Continue singing your tune. Your voice is who you are, and you deserve to be heard.

Truth- your truth- matters. Please don't hold back.

The world is waiting to hear you speak.

Peace,

Ayesha

Own your magic.

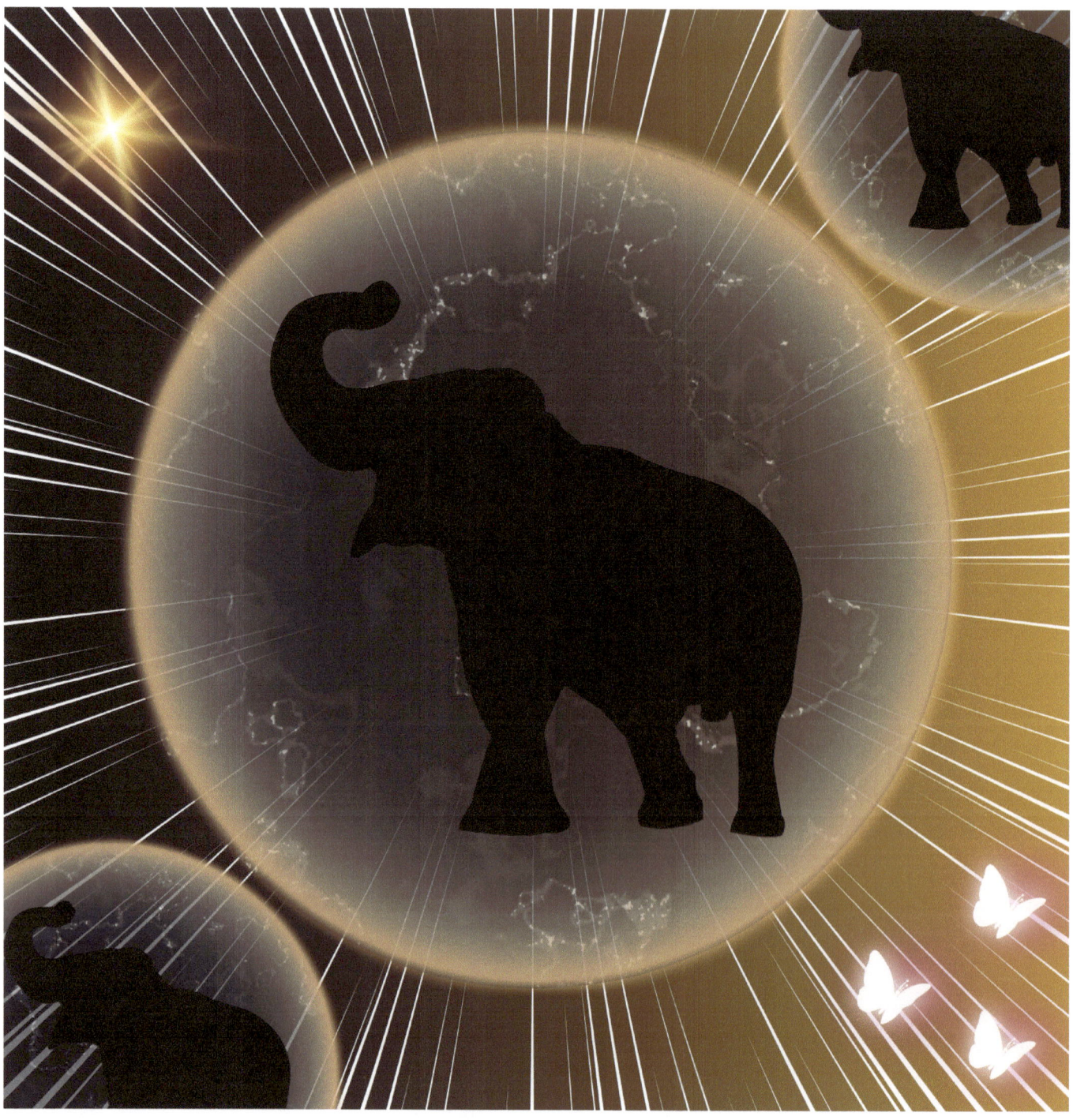

All was well in Zoranland. Nobody paid attention to their neighbors or the latest gossip. No news from the outside world entered Zoranland, and because everyone's hobbies in the town included keeping to themselves, there was not any news to get out. So, the world within and outside of Zoranland remained an untouched thought.

In fact, Zoranland was invisible to the eye for all but those who lived there. These residents were known as the Zains- an ancient elephant dynasty far removed from being defined as a tribe.

It was known that before the Zains inhabited Zoranland, years of conflict within their group resulted in the Zains breaking apart into their own, individual tribes, which ignited tensions that threatened their collective extinction.

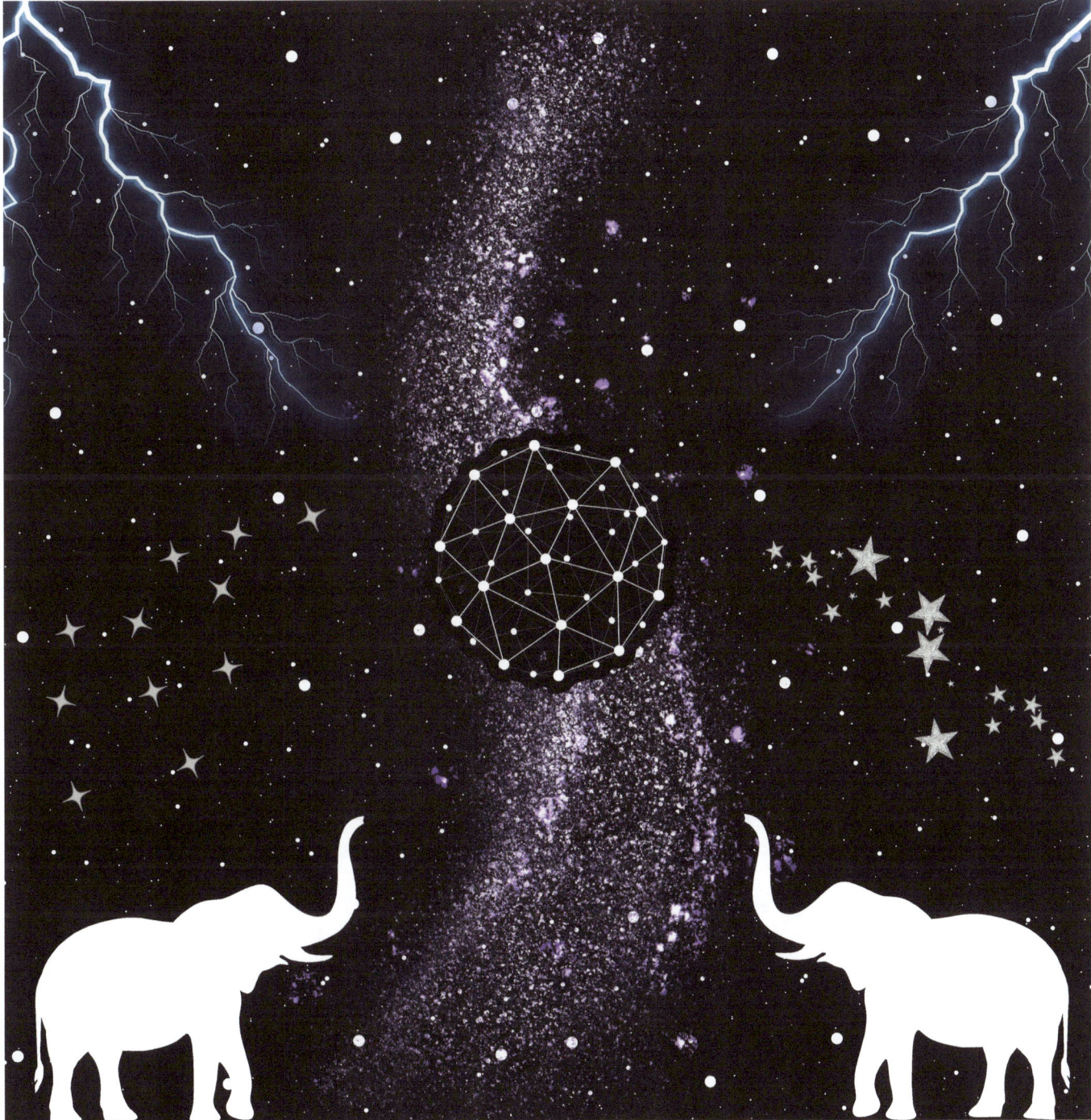

As a result, the creation of Zoranland provided the space for each member to live independently- without any interaction with others, which took away the need to form an identity around a tribe.

Now, all was peaceful, so all was well.
But not for Blue.

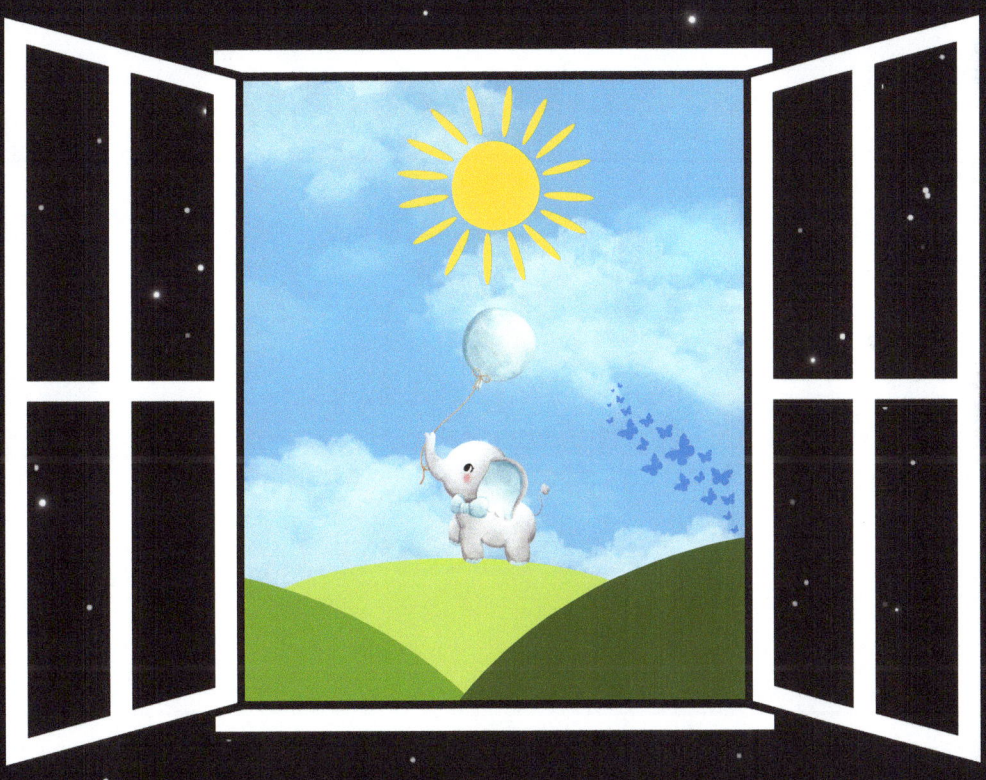

Blue was also absorbed in her own

bubble, but in a different way.

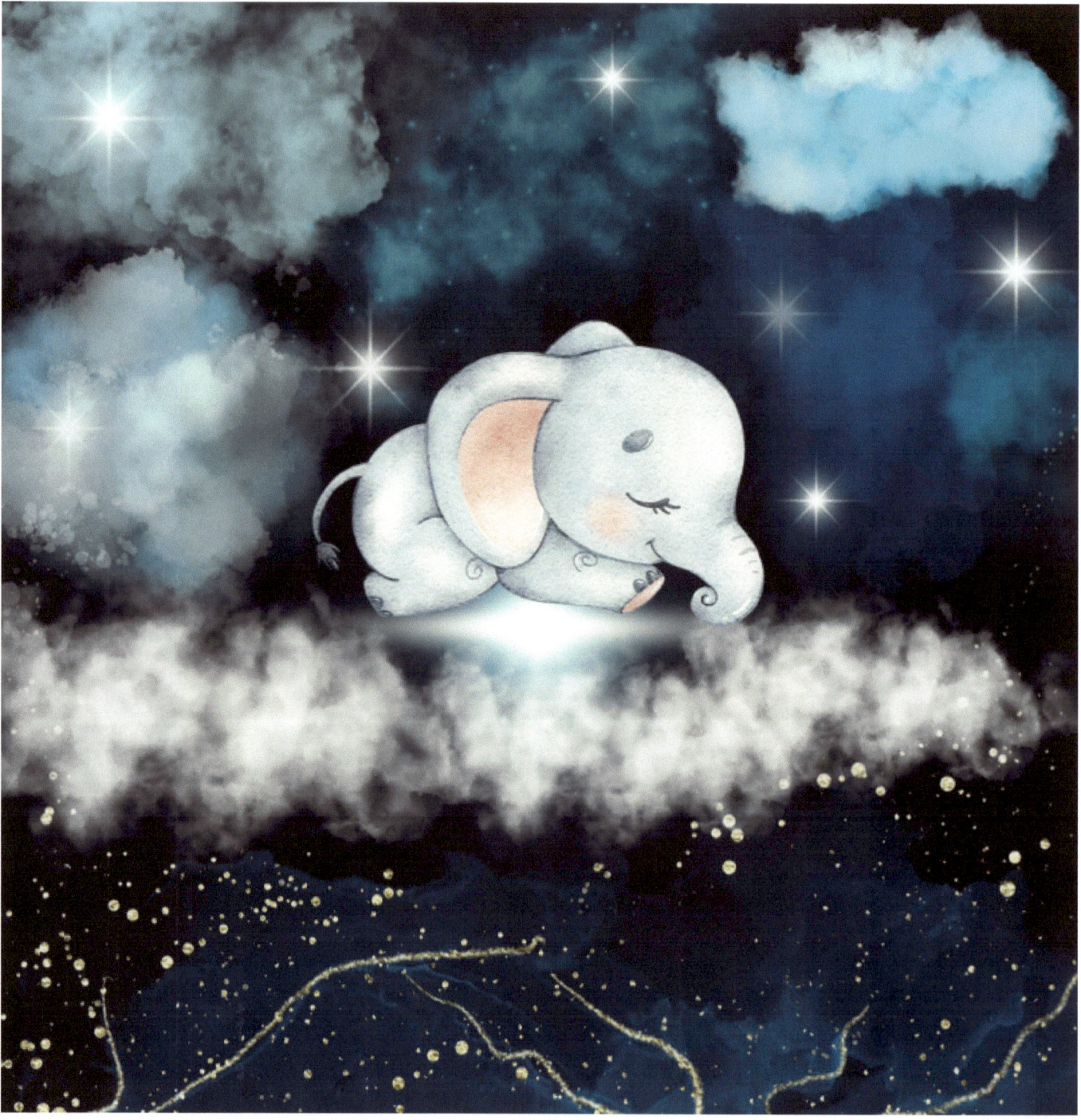

Despite Zoranland's intention to liberate individuals by monitoring only themselves, Blue did not feel free. Blue found herself feeling frequently disheartened by the disconnect she felt from the other elephants. She felt a desire to share her daydreams, for example, but she had an inkling that this behavior would feel too foreign, and therefore wrong, to the Zains.

Regardless of the isolation Blue felt between herself and the other elephants, there was still a spark within Blue that anchored her to a belief that the right moment would illuminate the way for her clan to rebuild a connection.

The thought of the Zains bonding with one another felt right. Blue liked that feeling of joy that she felt inside, and she recognized that she had a voice and a mind that could help remind her of that feeling.

Most importantly, as Blue would come to learn, her voice and her mind would always remain hers. Both could grow, but neither could close.

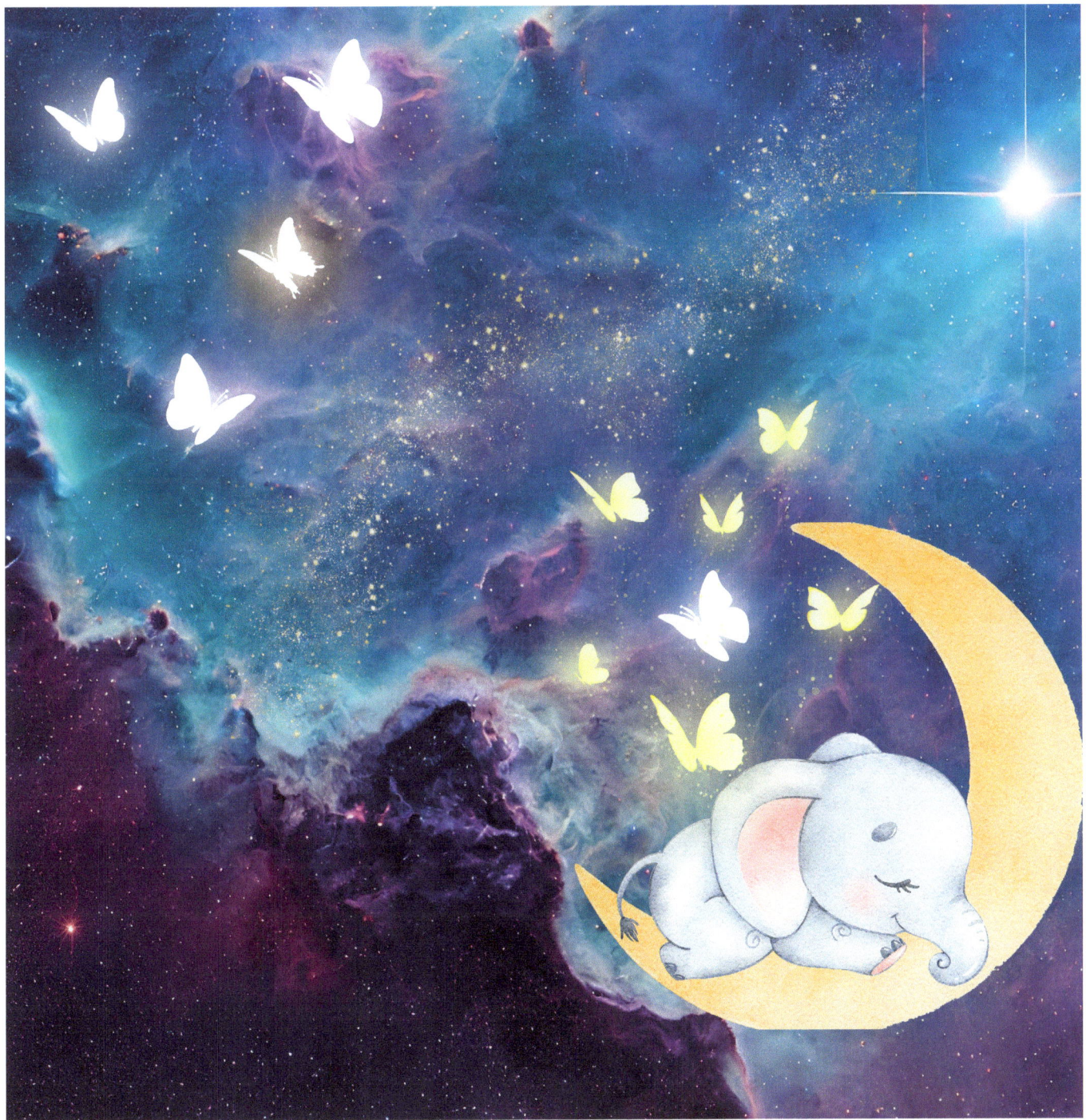

Along the way, Blue would choose to entertain this joyful thought in her mind amongst all of her other desires.

Blue could usually be found engaging these daydreams in her favorite spot in town, which happened to be the tallest peak in Zoranland. It was high enough to see the holographic stars as they subtly glitched with a flicker before yielding to a static dim. Blue never saw the lusterless stars as a sign of hopelessness, but rather, an opportunity.

Perhaps this was Blue's most distinct feature from the rest of the Zains, because Blue was aware of a magic she could access. In fact, she was unaware that the other elephants were completely oblivious to these powers.

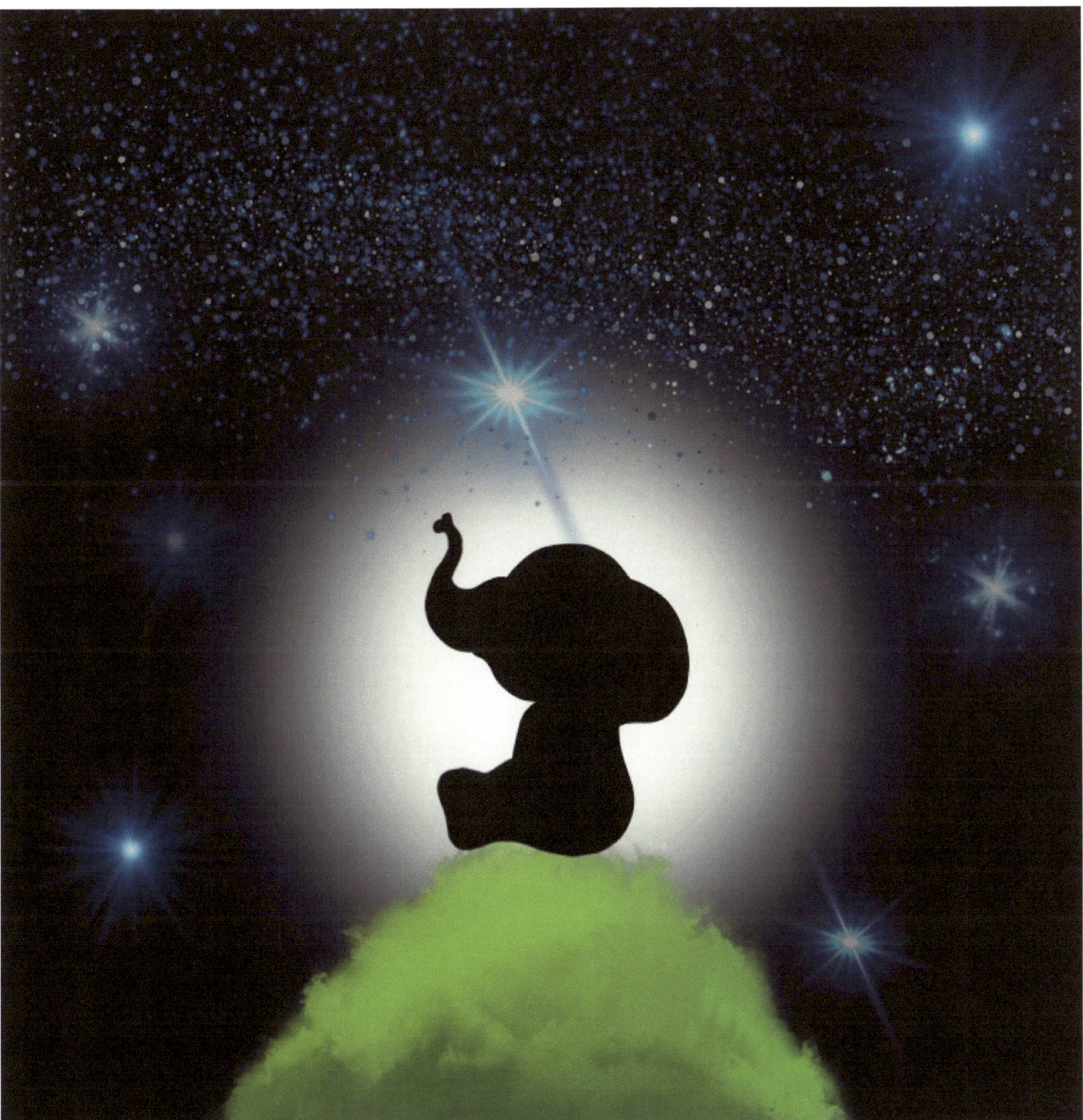

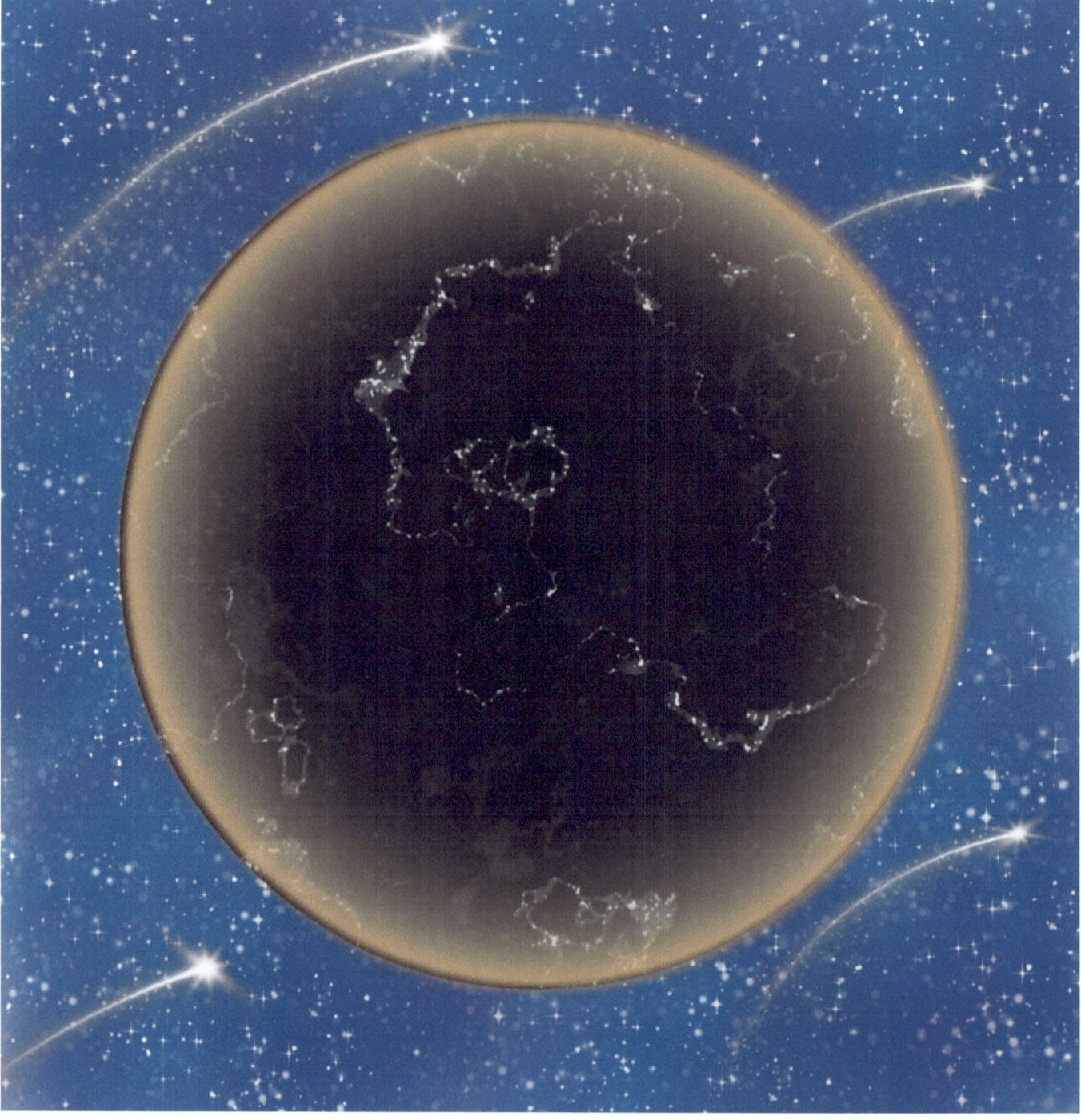

Blue used magic to cast comets into the sky she sought to

enliven, making innocent wishes that would often come true.

She had made previous, lackadaisical attempts towards her

biggest wish- the opportunity to see the world- but despite her

inner certainty that the day would come, Blue's belief that she

had to wait for the perfect time created an unconscious sense

of doubt when wishing upon a shooting star.

Her hesitation prevented her from recognizing that *she was*

worthy enough to request her heart-filled dream immediately.

That was, until one particular night.

Blue settled into her bottom-imprinted seat on the hilltop. She listened to the oscillating hum of the robotic trees and mechanical flowers operating all around her. As she cast her first comet into the cobalt sky, she became acutely aware of the magical sensation welling within her. With her next exhale, she watched as this miraculous feeling left her body and transformed the sky.

The shooting stars come from me! I am in control of my own magic!

The freedom and peace Blue often engaged in her mind flooded her whole body, and she suddenly became aware of a sense of confidence in trusting the magic within.

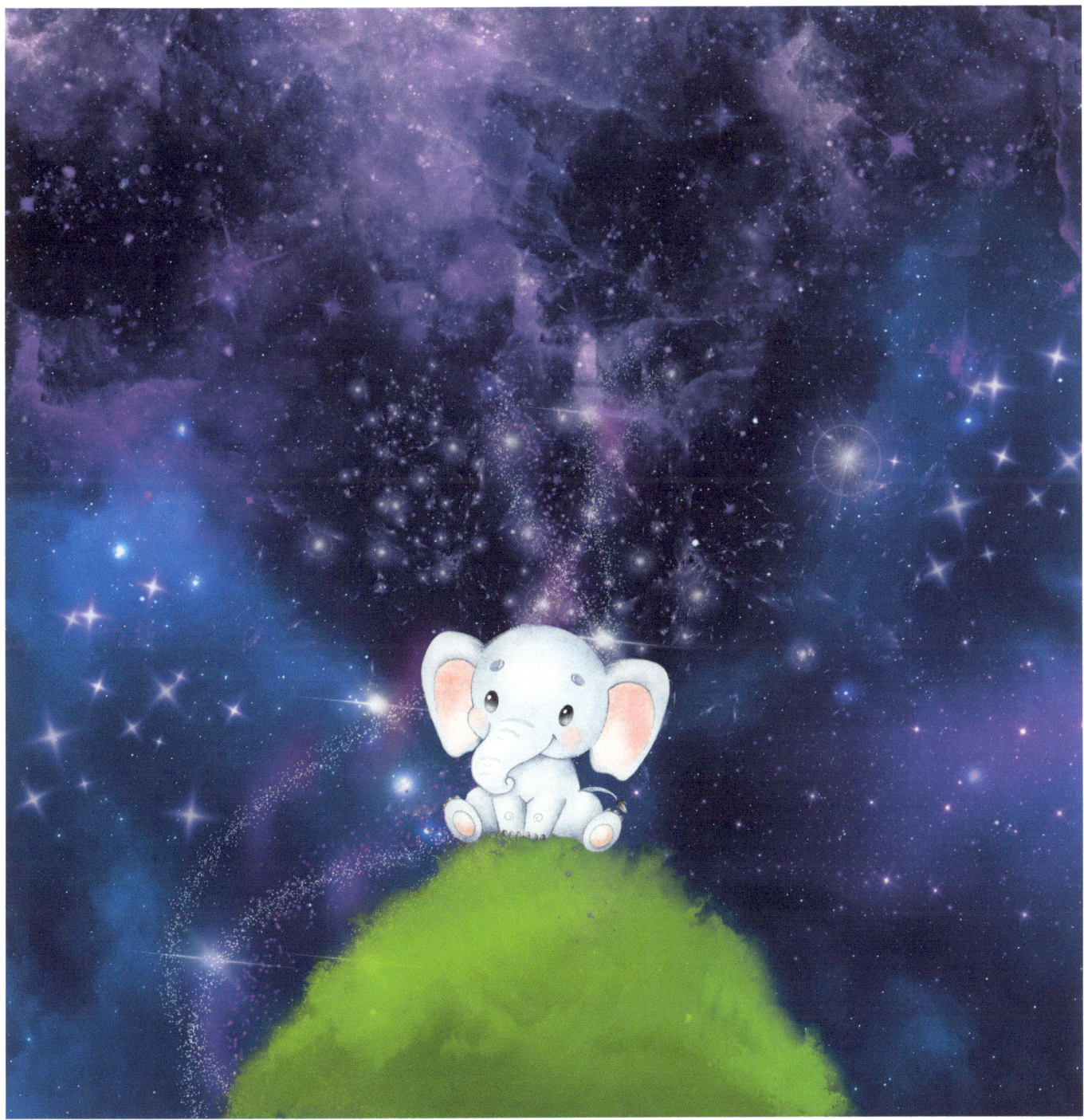

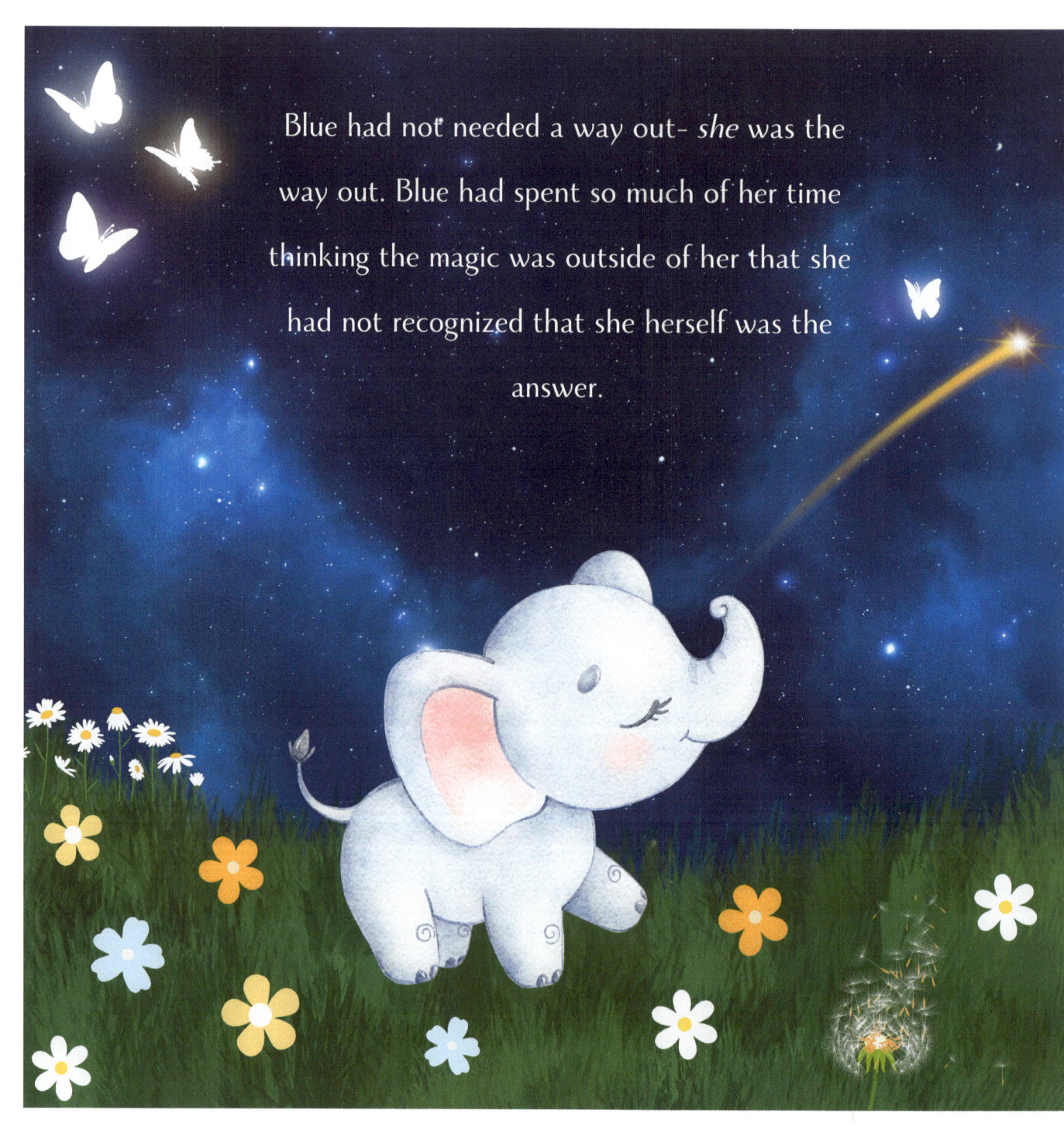

Blue had not needed a way out- *she* was the way out. Blue had spent so much of her time thinking the magic was outside of her that she had not recognized that she herself was the answer.

Blue's realization triggered a liberation within herself and the world surrounding her. As she honored her own, internal life force, she suddenly became aware of the external world she was a part of. The dim sky began to grow and glow brighter than ever. She watched Zoranland's round, holographic walls fade away and unite with the outside world. Below, her feet gripped grass- enabling her to know the trusted support of the earth below.

As Blue inhaled life, she released it to all of the life around her. The trees and flowers swayed in a gentle, calming breath. All of the plants had a prance about them. Blue was so mesmerized by the grace and playfulness her old friends had. There was a sense of emancipation in the air for everything. All really did feel well.

As Blue continued sitting on the hill, watching her world unfold and unite with the land around her, she began feeling the presence of all of the residents in her town. They all approached in sync. They all approached with awareness. Blue was ecstatic to see all of them there, but she was not surprised. They all watched in awe, they all watched in harmony, at Blue's presence. Her recognition and awareness of herself was the precipitator for all of the other elephants to feel seen, which enabled them to see themselves. And in doing so, the elephants were able to see their own magic that they possessed in this enchanted world.

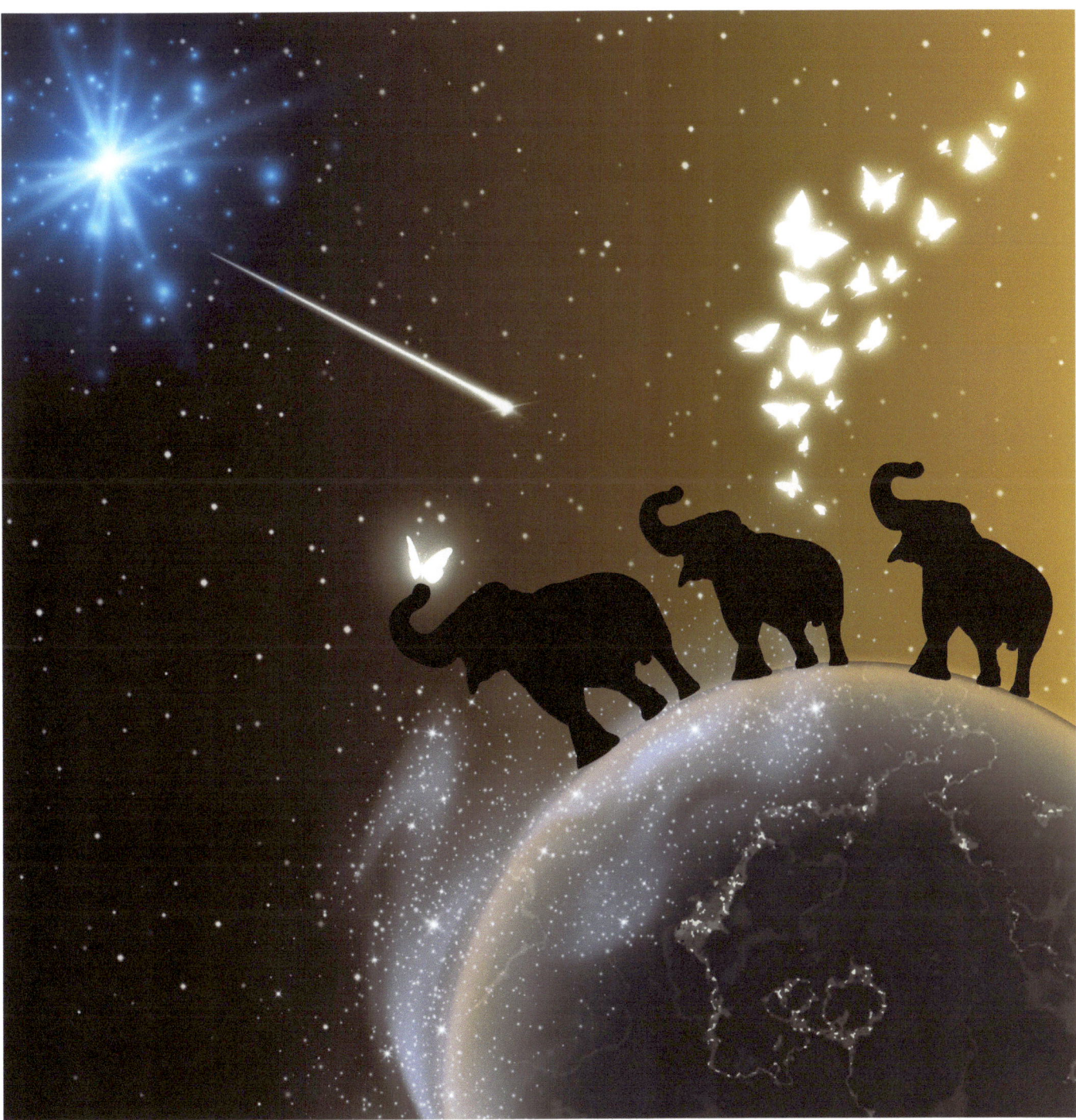

Blue's unknowing leadership did not stop there, however. As she merged with the outside world, her joyful spirit continued blooming. Blue had always been led to travel and explore the world, and now she was finally able to. She trotted around the new scenery, observing and noting all of the wonders before her. As Blue wandered beamingly, she sang:

"I don't quite know how to get there,
I don't quite know where to be,
But I'm going somewhere.
Somewhere great, indeed!"

Her voice echoed throughout the towns and so did her contagious energy. Blue's vivacious persona soared through the minds and hearts of all of those around her. As Blue stood in her own powers, she became the solution Zorandland had been built for. Perhaps the elephants outside of the Zains didn't possess mystical powers, but they were granted the strength to see their own worth and mental power.

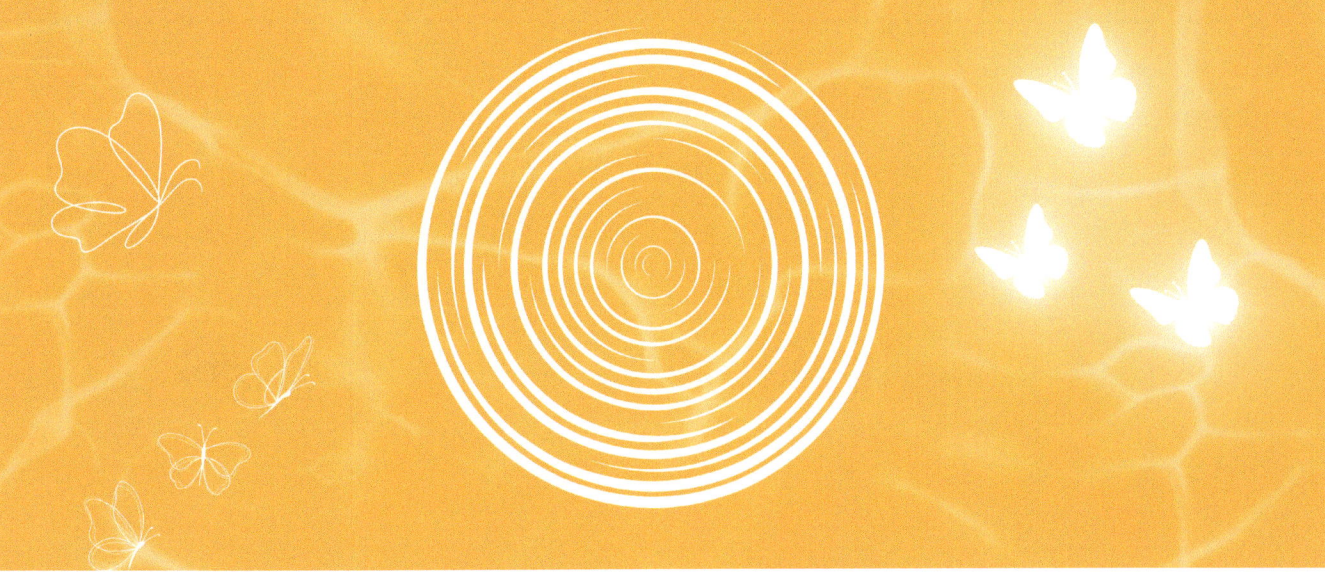

As the other elephant tribes grew in self-recognition and self-appreciation, they also grew in self-reliance. From healing illnesses to moving forward from mental setbacks, they grew in a profound understanding of their capabilities. By acknowledging themselves at the core, they were able to maneuver the world in a much more present and wholehearted manner. As a result, that essence is what they attracted.

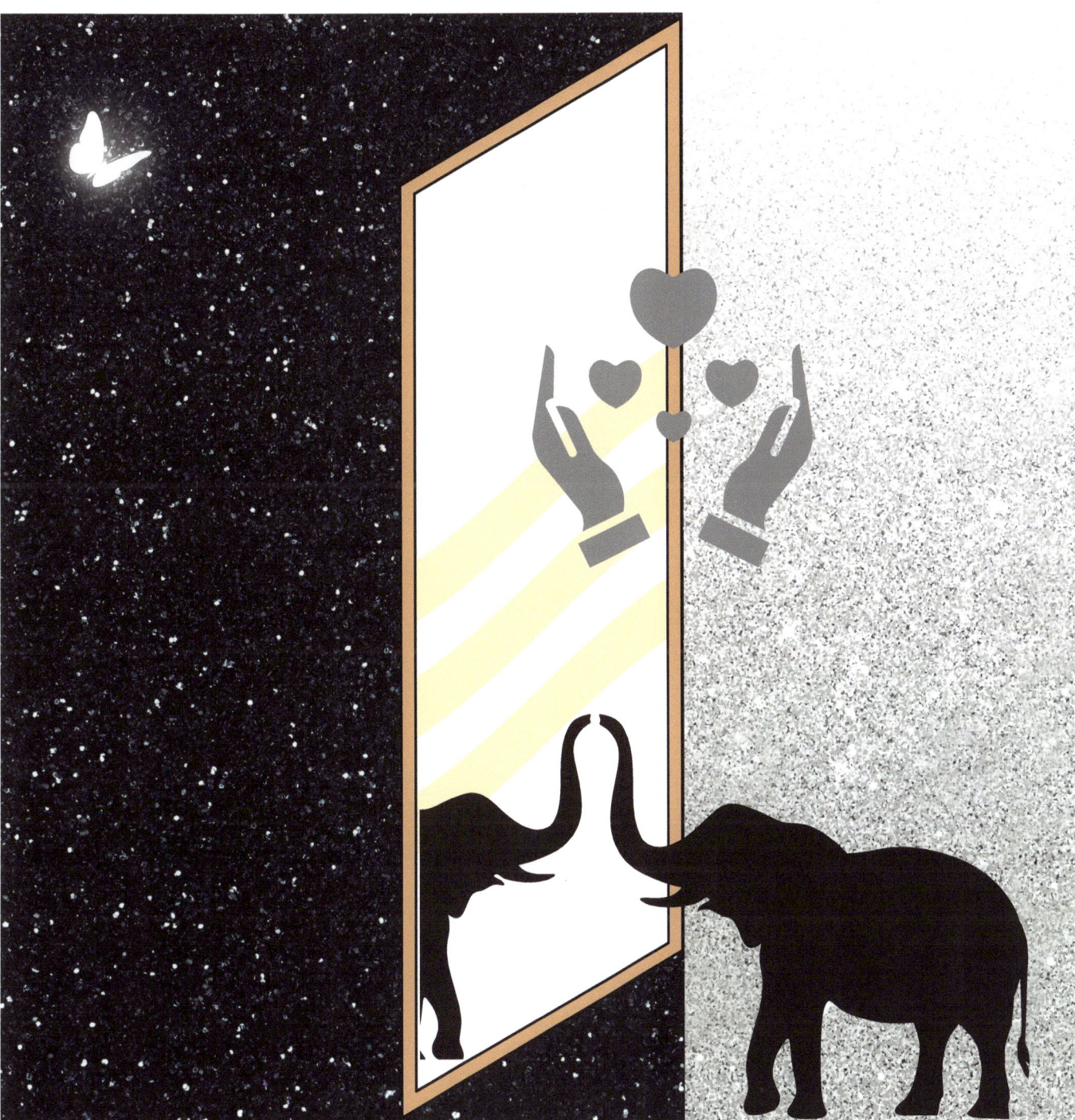

It only took one community member standing in her truth to empower others in embracing their truth as well. One spirit, one passion, and one's own belief in herself changed the way those around her viewed themselves.

As Blue allowed herself to be led by her heart, her explorative character enabled her to know where to go. As she let her enjoyment guide her, Blue found other paths present themselves to her. Blue found a love for filmmaking and creating documentaries wherever she went. She noticed that this medium granted her the support of the whole world, because everything had a role in her eye. Nothing was out of Blue's control, and everything was within her reach. Her cinematic eye attracted the masses, and Blue found herself being a reminder of joy to the entire world.

Blue's only obligation had been to see herself the way she saw the rest of the world. By permitting herself to be there for herself, Blue saw that the world was already ready to support her as well.

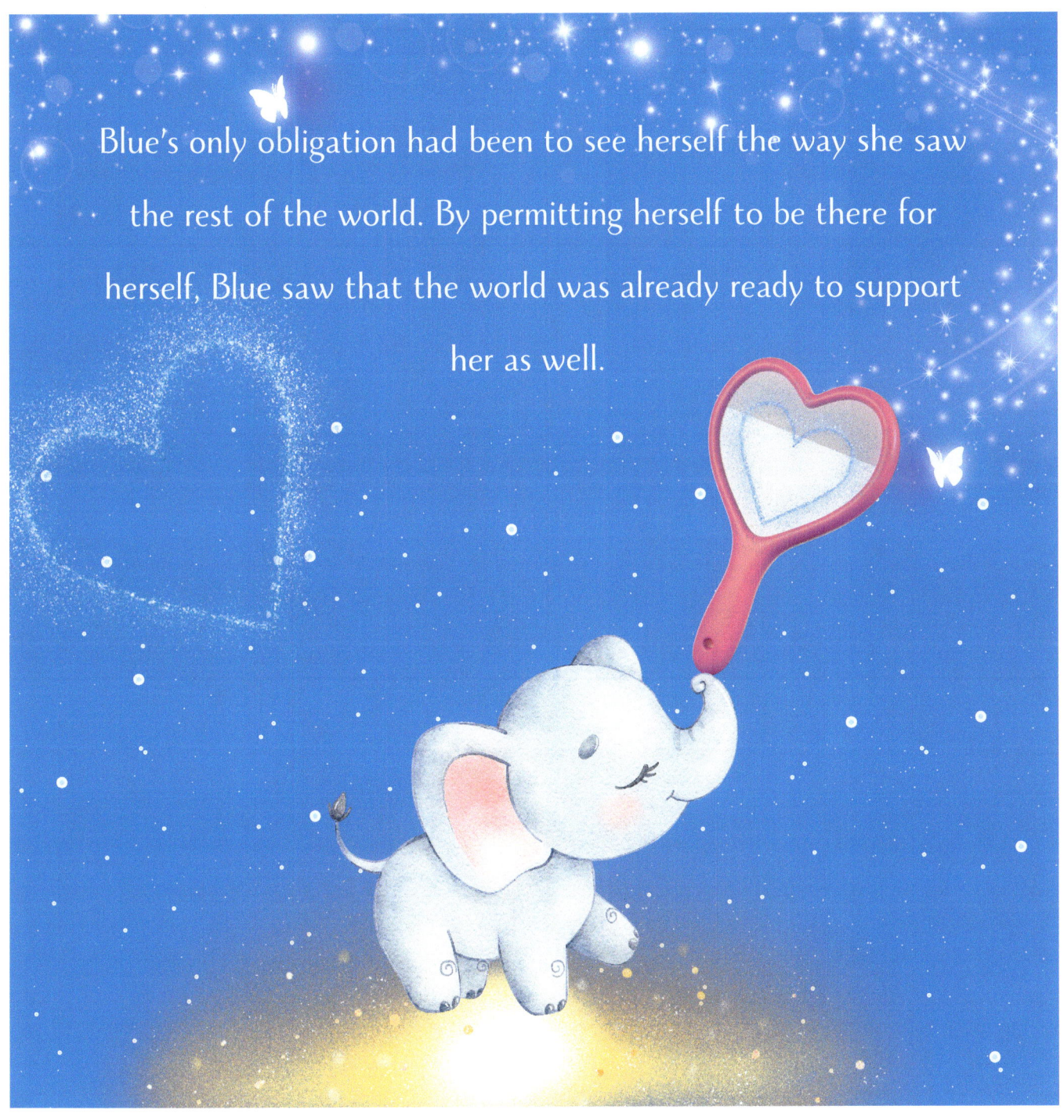

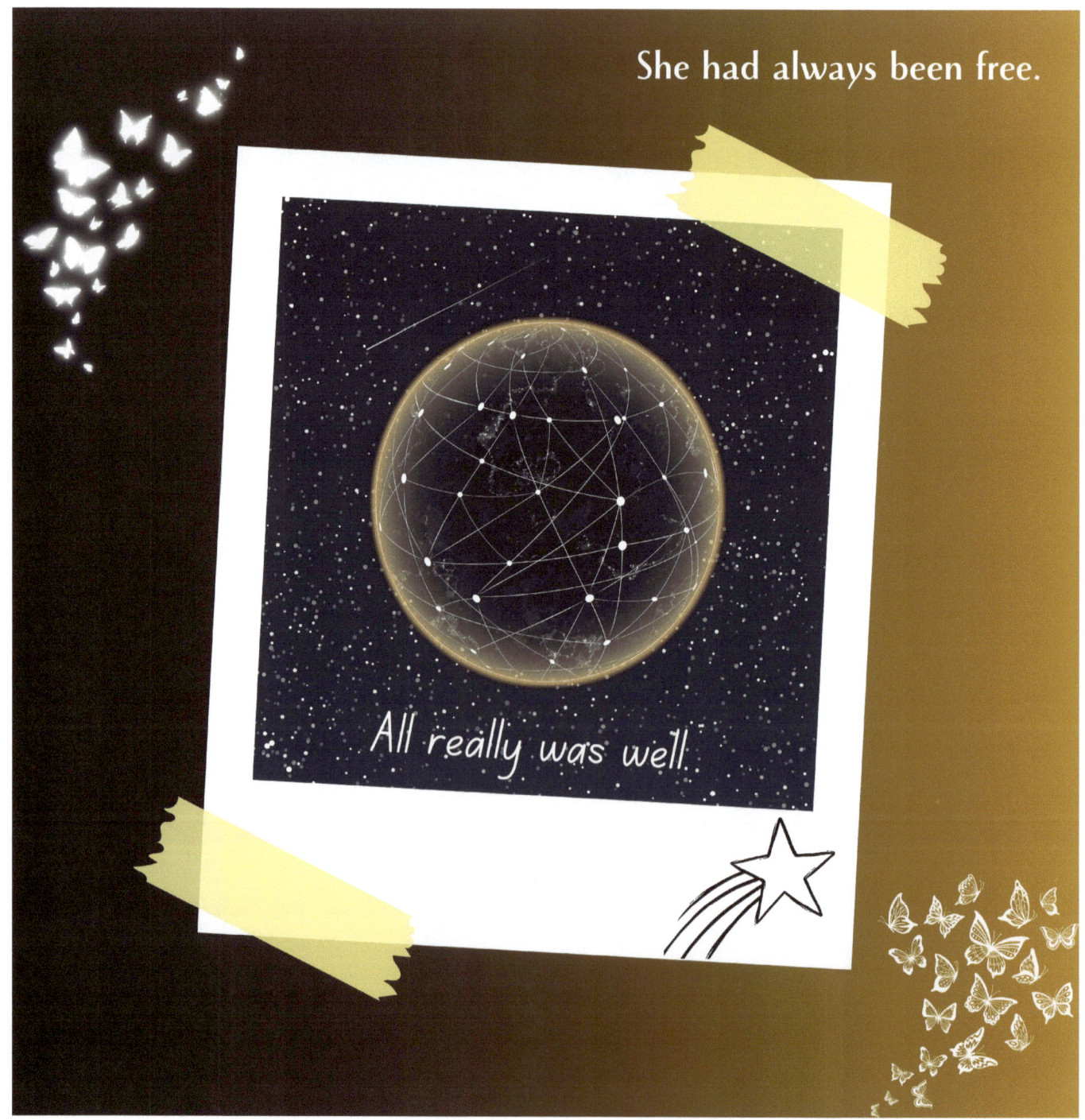

She had always been free.

All really was well

About Ayesha

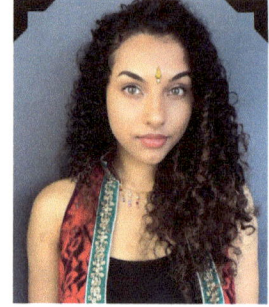

Ayesha is a multifaceted artist, speaker, goofball, and founder of Soul Volume, from Atlanta, GA. Her most explored mediums include acting, music, writing, photography, and movement.

Ayesha is a graduate from NYU Gallatin School of Individualized Study where she forged her concentration around the questions:

How do we identify, return to, and liberate the true self through returning to body consciousness, and how can that ignite global change?

Further, how can self-inquiry through embodied artistry release systemic trauma patterns, such as those caused by normalized racism and sexism?

Regarding her personal mission, whether it's performing, working with children in education, or creating worlds with her artistic projects, Ayesha's aim is to dismantle the current power structures and conditioning we have in place that hinder our permission, freedom, and safety to feel liberated and connected to ourselves, each other, and the world around us.

Ayesha is also passionate about chocolate chip cookies and locking herself in the bathroom for hours to recklessly dance to music.

To connect with Ayesha or follow her journey, she invites you to explore her community: SoulVolume.com

Author's Note (short and sweet)

I initially wrote this as a gift that I shared with loved ones over the past few years. Although this book is not my typical writing style, my intention was to appeal to the youthful spirit within by exploring the simplistic design of a children's book, while layering it with as many messages one wishes to extract. I wanted to create something that could be light enough to ease the mind, but grounded enough to speak to the inner child that may need the occasional reminder that their truth, presence, and inner magic are necessary in the world. I hope this supports an encouragement and safety in connecting to joyful alignment.

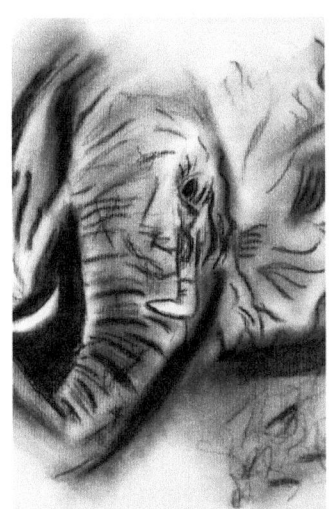

Author's Note (long... but passionate)

<u>Human Connection, Divine Intervention, Artistic Ascension</u>

Human connection, soul reflection. Fractals of a whole. What roots me profoundly in this continuous linkage of the matters that inspire me most emanate from human connection. I haven't always accepted this, because the zest I find stargazing on a solitary night hike, the rejuvenation of going for a run amidst a desolate downpour, and my fuel for art... I thought required less socialization and more intentional isolation.

Now, I recognize that the presence I feel in the privacy of nature, or the internal unearthing needed to express myself through physical, emotional, and spiritual art begins with my care- my necessity and appreciation- for overall human connection.

The presence of, the lack of, interacting in the human form with the human form is what sparks my drive and heightens my unification with a joyous and loving vibration. The privilege to meld with others unveils myself to myself. Connection is my tether to act through love so that my actions know love. Human connection is my reminder to continuously expand my perspective- my consciousness and awareness- and to receive the infinite beauty that awaits our attention.

We are all one large art piece. I move to the music left by others, I write from the emotional triggers I face by interacting with people, I am able to perform by taking in human behavior.

I get to create from what others have created through what sparked something in them. Human interaction is and forms one, infinitely expanding work of art. If art is a curator for my existence, it is inevitable that I must honor the essential root that is connection.

Understanding chaotic peace, understanding euphoric laughter, abysmal loneliness... these elements in human nature guide me to connect with source to find a groundedness with this teacher. The polarity of connection and isolation inspires me to dive within myself to reach a universal union that reveres the coexistence of separation and togetherness.

The human experience reveals all that is within. Our innate alliance with the inner and outer world respectively is an evolving body, which makes us inevitable, creative collaborators. It constructs the dualistic intertwinement of narrative and sensorial experiences. The presence of human connection as a way to see ourselves illuminates the seed of existence, passion, purpose, and the strength to accept all natures within... while embarking on the journey with love and play.

Human connection, divine intervention, artistic ascension, means we unavoidably fabricate this constant reinvention to illuminate our journey as one human extension.

21 November, 2021

www.ingramcontent.com/pod-product-compliance
Lightning Source LLC
Chambersburg PA
CBHW042028230526
45474CB00006B/49